BIBLE AFFIRMATIONS FOR BLACK MEN IN 2024

Bible Affirmations for black men to achieve success, Navigate Challenges and become a true king.

ANDRE TAYLOR

Table of contents

INTRODUCTION

Brother, close your eyes. Feel the sun-kissed melanin of your skin, a testament to generations bathed in the glory of creation. Inhale deeply, and sense the fire within – the embers of a king waiting to erupt. You are not just a man, you are a force, a potential waiting to be unleashed. The path to claim your crown may be strewn with challenges—doubts whispering, and the world attempting to dim your light. This book is your shield and sword, guiding you on the journey to unlock your true royal identity.

What exactly are Affirmations?

Affirmations are the alchemy of language, the transformative incantations that shape the fabric of our reality. They are not mere words; they are the resonance of intent, the echoes of the soul reaching out to the universe. In their essence, affirmations are a deliberate and conscious practice of molding thoughts into powerful declarations that influence our perception, actions, and, ultimately, our destiny.

Picture affirmations as seeds planted in the fertile soil of the mind. Each word, each phrase, carries the potential to blossom into a reality that aligns with our deepest desires. They are the whispers of self-love, the symphony of positivity that counteracts the dissonance of doubt. Affirmations are the brushes with which we paint our mental landscape, crafting a masterpiece that reflects the colors of our aspirations.

At their core, affirmations are an intimate conversation with the self. They invite us to challenge limiting beliefs, rewrite the narratives of self-doubt, and sculpt a self-image that radiates with confidence. In the vast tapestry of existence, affirmations are the threads that weave resilience, fortitude, and unwavering faith into the very fabric of our being.

Yet, their potency transcends the individual. Affirmations possess a collective energy, resonating with the cosmos and echoing the aspirations of communities and cultures. In the context of "BIBLE AFFIRMATIONS FOR BLACK MEN IN 2024," they become a bridge between ancient wisdom and contemporary struggles, empowering individuals to navigate the complexities of the world with grace, strength, and a profound sense of purpose.

So, affirmations are not just words; they are the conduits of transformation, the keys to unlocking the dormant potential within us. They are the sacred language of self-creation, enabling us to sculpt a reality that aligns with the highest vision of who we are and who we aspire to become.

Purpose and Relevance of Affirmations for Black Men

In the pulsating rhythm of the year, the purpose of this book beats with a heart attuned to the aspirations, struggles, and triumphs of Black men. This isn't just a collection of affirmations; it's a lifeline, a narrative that resonates with the unique experiences woven into the tapestry of Black identity.

In a world that constantly evolves, the relevance of these affirmations becomes a beacon of guidance. We stand at the crossroads of progress and challenge, and this book serves as a compass, pointing toward the empowerment of Black men. It acknowledges the daily battles faced – the systemic hurdles, the echoes of history, and the ever-present need for strength.

"Bible affirmations for Black Men in 2024" is a rallying cry, reminding you of your inherent worth, resilience, and capability. It's not just about facing the challenges of today; it's about embracing a future where success is not a distant dream but an achievable reality.

This book speaks to the soul of the Black experience, affirming that your story is not only valid but powerful. It seeks to create a space where aspirations flourish, where the echoes of ancestors reverberate, and where the journey toward becoming a true king is both celebrated and navigated with wisdom from the ages.

In the context of your life as a Black man, these affirmations become powerful tools against negativity and stereotypes that might hinder your progress. They transform into armor, protecting your spirit from doubt and fear. Moreover, they act as a compass, guiding you toward the realization of your dreams and the fulfillment of your God-given potential.

Remember, affirmations aren't magic spells; they demand commitment, intention, and an unwavering belief in yourself and God's promises.

This book provides you with the knowledge, practical tools, and, most importantly, the faith to embark on a transformative journey.

Together, let's explore the scriptures, discovering how verses like **Joshua 1:9** resonate: "Be strong and courageous. Do not be afraid; do not be discouraged, for the Lord your God will be with you wherever you go." In simpler terms, find strength and courage, fear not, be undeterred, for the Lord your God accompanies you on every step of your journey.

CHAPTER 1: Unearthing the King Within

Brother, ever felt that flicker of greatness within you, that spark of something powerful waiting to be unleashed? That, my friend, is the king waiting to be crowned. But before you ascend your throne, a journey awaits, a journey of self-discovery fueled by the very word of God.

Discovering the Power of God's Word for Transformation

The Bible isn't just a dusty tome collecting on a shelf; it's a pulsating force, a living testament to the transformative power of the divine. Imagine, brother, the moment creation itself sparked forth at the utterance of God's word. That same power lies dormant within you, waiting to be ignited. Affirmations are the flint you strike against the steel of scripture, the spark that sets your potential ablaze.

Think of affirmations as royal decrees, not mere wishes. When you declare, "I am fearfully and wonderfully made, created in the image of God **(Psalm 139:14),"** you aren't just parroting words; you are wielding the power of the divine, sculpting your self-image into a masterpiece. Imagine reciting with conviction, "With God all things are possible **(Matthew 19:26),"** and feeling the shackles of doubt melt away, replaced by an unwavering belief in your ability to conquer any obstacle. These are not just affirmations; they are war cries, battle hymns echoing through the chambers of your soul, reminding you of your inherent power and divinely ordained potential.

Why Affirmations Matter for Black Men

Brother, you walk a path illuminated yet shadowed. The world throws its shade, whispers doubt, and tries to clip your wings. Systemic barriers like barbed wire fences, negative stereotypes like venomous darts, societal expectations like suffocating smog – these forces conspire to dim your light. But affirmations are your shield, your sun-forged armor deflecting negativity. They are the clarion call that pierces the fog of self-doubt, reminding you of who you truly are – a king, a descendant of greatness, a man divinely appointed for purpose.

Affirmations are not magic spells, but they are weapons in the fight for your rightful place. They are the antidote to the poison of self-deprecation, the compass guiding you towards a life that reflects God's plan. They are your declaration of self-worth, a thunderous roar challenging the external forces that seek to define you.

Breaking Free from Limiting Beliefs

We all carry burdens, invisible chains forged from limiting beliefs – thoughts ingrained over time that whisper "not good enough," "not strong enough," "not worthy enough." But remember, brother, your mind is not a prison, but a fertile ground waiting to be cultivated with the seeds of truth. Scripture is the divine gardener, its words weeding out the poisonous thoughts and planting empowering affirmations.

We all carry burdens, invisible chains forged from limiting beliefs – thoughts ingrained over time that whisper "not good enough," "not strong enough," "not worthy enough." But remember, brother, your mind is not a prison, but a fertile ground waiting to be cultivated with the seeds of truth. Scripture is the divine gardener, its words weeding out the poisonous thoughts and planting empowering affirmations.

Envision exchanging the falsehood of "I am insignificant" with the profound truth found in Jeremiah 29:11, which assures that God's thoughts toward you are filled with peace and hope, not harm, offering a promising future. Experience the alleviation of self-doubt as you reflect on empowering verses like Philippians 4:13, acknowledging that through Christ's strength, you can accomplish all things. By incorporating scripture into your affirmations, you engage in a continuous process of mind renewal, dismantling the mental barriers that hold you back and paving the way for a kingly mindset

Embracing Your Black Identity

Your Black skin is not a burden, but a crown, a tapestry woven by the divine hand itself. It's a testament to resilience, a badge of honor forged in the fires of history. Yet, the world may try to convince you otherwise, whispering narratives of inferiority and inadequacy. But affirmations become your battle cry, reminding you of the strength, wisdom, and unique perspective embedded within your very being.

Declare with conviction
• "I am strong, resilient, and capable, a descendant of a lineage blessed by God."
• "My Black skin is a beacon of light, reflecting the beauty and diversity of God's creation."
• "I walk with purpose, carrying the torch of my ancestors and illuminating the path for future generations."

These affirmations are not just about self-love; they are about reclaiming your narrative, owning your God-given identity, and recognizing the power that lies dormant within.

Remember, brother, this is just the first step on your journey to claiming your crown.

CHAPTER 2: Exploring Your Innate Potential Endowed by God

Dear brother, envision peering into a mirror that doesn't reflect limitations but instead showcases your potential. Yet, not just any potential—this is the dormant, God-given reservoir within you, awaiting release. In this chapter, let's embark on a journey of self-discovery, unveiling the strengths, virtues, and resilience intricately woven into the fabric of your existence.

Revealing Your Strengths and Virtues through Scripture

The Bible transcends mere stories; it's a profound source of wisdom, unveiling the strengths and virtues woven into God's creations. Consider David, the shepherd who confronted a giant with unwavering faith. He wasn't born a warrior, but his courage and God-given potential lay in wait to be revealed. Similarly, dear brother, unique strengths reside within you, ready to be unearthed.

Refer to scripture as your compass

Proverbs 31:25: "Strength and honor are her clothing; she shall rejoice in time to come." Ponder on your inner strength, recognizing it's not about physical prowess but the steadfast spirit enabling you to face challenges with dignity.

Romans 12:6-8: "Having gifts that differ according to the grace given to us, let us use them:... if it is to encourage, let him encourage; if it is to contribute, let him contribute generously; if it is to lead, let him do so with zeal; if it is to show mercy, let him do so cheerfully." Identify your unique gifts, acknowledging they are not for personal gain but for the service and upliftment of others.

• Affirmation: "I am more than a man; I am a descendant of kings, inheriting strength, resilience, and wisdom from generations past."
• Affirmation: "My distinct talents and gifts are not for personal gain but instruments to uplift and empower my community."
• Affirmation: "With each passing day, I delve deeper into scripture, unveiling the concealed treasures of my potential."

By meditating on verses like these and incorporating them into your affirmations, you unlock the inherent potential that has always resided within you.

Overcoming Challenges with Biblical Wisdom

Life presents challenges, brother. Obstacles will surface, doubts will whisper, and the path may appear unclear. Yet, remember, even the mightiest oak began as a tiny acorn, weathering storms and growing stronger with each challenge. Scripture imparts timeless wisdom to navigate these hurdles:

The book of Joshua chapter 1 verse 9 encourages strength and courage, reassuring that God is always with you, so there's no need to fear or be discouraged in any circumstance. In moments of fear, repeat this verse, sensing God's strength flowing through you.

The book of James chapter 2 verse 1 to 4 advises finding joy in trials, as they strengthen faith, build endurance, and contribute to personal perfection and completeness. Challenges are not punishments; instead, they offer chances to shape your character and nurture unwavering faith.

- **Affirmation:** "When fear whispers, I recall the Lord's promise: 'Do not be afraid; do not be discouraged.' His hand guides me through any storm."

- **Affirmation:** "Challenges are not punishments but opportunities to refine my character and build an unshakeable faith."
- **Affirmation:** "With each trial overcome, I emerge stronger, more resilient, and closer to fulfilling my true potential."

Becoming the Optimal Version of Yourself

Stagnation isn't an option, brother. Like a river carving its path through stone, you are meant to continually flow, evolve, and become the best version of yourself. How do you navigate this journey? Turn to scripture as your guiding map:

The book of Philippians chapter 3 verse 12 to 14 expresses the pursuit of spiritual growth, acknowledging imperfection but striving forward with determination. The focus is on leaving the past behind and striving towards the goal set by God in Christ Jesus. This verse reminds you that growth is a lifelong journey, not a destination. Celebrate your progress, but never settle for complacency.

The book of Proverbs chapter 22 verse 29 emphasizes that a skilled individual in their work will gain recognition, standing before kings rather than being unnoticed. Pursue excellence in all you do, not for personal gain but to glorify God and inspire others.

- **Affirmation:** "Growth is a lifelong journey, not a destination. I celebrate my progress while continuously striving towards the best version of myself."
- **Affirmation:** "My pursuit of excellence is not for personal glory, but to glorify God and inspire others."
- **Affirmation:** "Guided by scripture and fueled by faith, I embark on a transformative journey of self-discovery and purpose."

Remember, becoming the best version of yourself is not a competition but about fulfilling the unique purpose God has designed for you.

By incorporating these verses into your affirmations and seeking guidance from scripture, you embark on a transformative journey of continuous growth, fueled by faith and the pursuit of excellence.

CHAPTER 3: Awakening the Warrior Within

Imagine, brother, not a crown perched atop your head, but a throne room blazing within your chest. This sanctuary, built of spirit, mind, and body, is the wellspring of your strength, the forge where you'll craft the warrior destined to claim your rightful place in the world. But before you raise your banner, you must awaken the king slumbering within, ignite the embers of potential waiting to be fanned into a roaring fire.

Spiritual Practices Rooted in Prayer and Reflection

Forget kneeling in supplication. Imagine standing toe-to-toe with the Divine, your voice not a whimper, but a battle cry echoing through the heavens. Prayer isn't a one-sided plea, but a forge where doubts are hammered into resolve, where anxieties are tempered into unwavering faith. Picture yourself, eyes blazing, heart pounding, not begging for favors, but forging your destiny with each fervent word.

Reflecting on the warrior-king David, the book of Psalm chapter 17 verse 6 highlights the earnest plea for God's attention in the midst of battle.

• **Affirmation:** With each roar of prayer, I sharpen my faith into an unyielding blade, ready to cleave through any obstacle.

Unveiling Your Inner Hero

In the chaos of daily life, introspection becomes a forgotten weapon. But just as a still pond reflects the vastness of the sky, moments of quiet reflection reveal the depths within you. Don't just react to the world's noise; silence the clamor and listen to the whispers of your soul. Contemplate the battles you've fought, the scars you bear with pride, and align your actions with the heroic destiny etched in your spirit. Let stillness be your whetstone, polishing the warrior within to a dazzling shine.

Drawing from the wisdom of Proverbs chapter 16 verse 9, it underscores that while humans may devise plans, ultimate victory is established by the Lord.

• **Affirmation:** In the quiet moments, I discover my true north, aligning my path with the divine purpose for my life.

Honoring Your Body with Healthful Habits

Your body isn't just a shell, brother, but a fortified citadel, meticulously crafted to house the warrior within. Treat it with the respect it deserves. Nourish it with foods that fuel your spirit, not dull it. Invigorate it with movement that hones your reflexes, not weakens them. Grant it the rest it craves, for a well-rested warrior is a formidable one, ready to conquer any challenge and claim any victory.

In line with Paul's teachings from first Corinthians chapter 6 verse 19 to 20, it emphasizes that the body is a sacred space for the Holy Spirit, a divine gift. It stresses that individuals, having been bought with a price, should honor God by respecting and caring for their bodies.

• **Affirmation:** I treat my body as the sacred temple of my warrior spirit, fueling it with strength and agility, honoring it as the foundation of my victories.

Building Emotional Resilience with Biblical Principles

Life throws curveballs, brother, and sometimes they come at you fast and furious. But like the ancient oak weathering relentless storms, you too can cultivate unwavering emotional resilience. Draw inspiration from the heroes of scripture, where David faced giants with unwavering courage and Joseph endured betrayal with unyielding dignity. Remember, challenges are not punishments, but opportunities to forge your emotional armor, to build walls of resilience that allow you to stand tall, even when the world seems to crumble around you.

Echoing James chapter 1 verse 2 to 4, it encourages finding joy in trials, recognizing that the challenges strengthen faith, cultivate perseverance, and contribute to achieving wholeness and completeness.

• **Affirmation:** With each challenge overcome, I emerge stronger, more resilient, my inner kingdom fortified against the slings and arrows of life.

CHAPTER 4:
Maintaining Your Reign

Staying Motivated and Achieving Your Goals with God's Grace

Imagine yourself, not adorned with a crown, but embodying its essence. The weight of leadership rests upon your shoulders, the responsibility to guide your kingdom towards prosperity and fulfillment. However, a true leader's power arises not from external symbols, but from the fire within – a fire fueled by purpose and faith. This chapter serves as your compass, guiding you to:

Uncovering Your Core Values and Passions Aligned with God's Will

Before embarking on your reign, delve deep into the treasure chest of your heart. Uncover the core values that define you, the passions that ignite your spirit. Ask yourself: what compels you to rise each day? What injustices stir your soul to action?

Remember, a kingdom built solely on ambition crumbles easily. Seek values that resonate with God's will, etching them onto your heart like guiding stars.

Micah 6:8 implores individuals to recognize the essence of goodness by emphasizing the Lord's simple requirements: to act justly, show mercy, and walk humbly in companionship with God.

• **Affirmation:** My values are the compass guiding my reign, ensuring my kingdom is built on righteousness and compassion, reflecting the divine will.

Crafting SMART Goals Guided by Scripture

Goals are not mere wishes whispered into the wind. They are the blueprints of your kingdom, the milestones on your path to greatness. But remember, even the most magnificent cathedral starts with a single, well-laid stone. Craft your goals using the SMART framework: Specific, Measurable, Achievable, Relevant, and Time-bound. Seek inspiration from scripture, where Nehemiah rebuilt Jerusalem brick by brick, fueled by faith.

Proverbs 29:18 underscores the importance of vision, stating that a lack of it leads to a decline, while those who adhere to the law find happiness

• **Affirmation:** My goals are not just aspirations, but meticulously crafted plans, guided by scripture and fueled by purpose, leading me towards a kingdom that reflects God's blessings.

Overcoming Challenges with Perseverance and Faith

No reign is without its difficulties. Doubts will whisper like chilling winds, setbacks will threaten to topple your resolve. But remember, even the most stalwart tree weathers countless storms, its roots growing stronger with each challenge. Embrace challenges as opportunities to refine your leadership, to build unshakeable faith. Draw strength from the perseverance of Job, who amidst immense suffering clung to his faith.

James 1:2-4 advises finding joy in trials, as they strengthen faith, build endurance, and contribute to personal perfection and completeness.

• **Affirmation:** Challenges are not roadblocks, but stepping stones on my journey. With steadfast faith and perseverance, I overcome obstacles, emerging stronger and more resilient.

Expressing Gratitude and Recognizing God's Blessings

A true leader doesn't just claim victories, but celebrates them with a grateful heart. Recognize the blessings bestowed upon you, the divine hand guiding your steps. Express gratitude not just in words, but in actions. Share your prosperity, uplift others, and let your kingdom be a beacon of hope for all. Remember, a grateful heart is a fertile ground for continued blessings.

Psalm 100:3-4 highlights recognizing the Lord as our Creator and acknowledging our belonging to Him. It encourages approaching God with gratitude and praise, emphasizing thankfulness and blessing His name.

• **Affirmation:** I acknowledge and celebrate the blessings in my life, expressing gratitude through my actions, fostering a kingdom that overflows with joy and reflects God's abundance.

Remember, building a kingdom is a journey, not a destination. There will be triumphs and trials, moments of doubt and days of dazzling glory. But through it all, hold fast to the values that light your path, Remember, the world needs your unique brand of leadership, your unwavering spirit, your kingdom built on love and light. Go forth and shine, brother. The world awaits your brilliance.

CHAPTER 5:
Nurturing Your
Inner Champion

Positive Declarations for Personal Growth Anchored in Scripture

Dear friend, envision not merely facing life's trials but actively overcoming them. Within you resides a warrior's spirit, ready to be unleashed, guided by the wisdom of scripture and the strength of self-confidence. This chapter provides you with the means to:

Enhance Confidence and Self-Worth

• Embrace your unique attributes: Reflect on your strengths, talents, and experiences, recognizing their value and contribution to the world.

Affirmation: Psalm 139:14 declares that I am fearfully and wonderfully made. I possess distinct gifts and talents meant to be shared with the world.

Challenge negative self-talk

Acknowledge self-doubt without dwelling on it. Replace negativity with affirmations emphasizing your worth and capabilities.

• **Affirmation**: I am capable and strong, worthy of achieving great things. I choose to silence negativity and trust in my abilities.

Step out of your comfort zone

Dare to try new things, even if they seem intimidating. Every success, big or small, boosts your confidence and broadens your potential.

• **Affirmation:** I courageously face new challenges, knowing that each step outside my comfort zone strengthens my confidence and opens doors to new possibilities.

Release Negative Thoughts

Identify the source of negativity: Understand the root cause, whether it's comparing yourself to others or dwelling on past failures, to effectively address it.

• **Affirmation**: I acknowledge the source of negativity within me and choose to let it go. I focus on the present moment and the positive possibilities that lie ahead.

Practice mindfulness

Meditation and mindfulness techniques help you become aware of negative thoughts without judgment, allowing you to release them gently.

- **Affirmation:** With each breath, I release negativity and find peace within myself. My mind is clear and calm, ready to embrace positivity.

Focus on the positive

Actively seek and appreciate the good things in your life, shifting your perspective towards optimism and gratitude.

- **Affirmation:** I choose to focus on the blessings in my life, big and small. Gratitude fills my heart, attracting more abundance and joy.

Cultivate Healthy Relationships

Practice active listening: Give others your full attention, showing genuine interest in their thoughts and feelings.

- **Affirmation**: I listen with an open heart and mind, understanding the perspectives and experiences of others. My relationships are built on mutual respect and empathy.

Communicate openly and honestly

Express your needs and desires clearly, while also being receptive to others' perspectives.

- **Affirmation:** I communicate with honesty and kindness, fostering healthy and open relationships filled with trust and understanding.

Offer support and encouragement
Build each other up with kind words and actions, fostering a sense of mutual respect and love.
- **Affirmation:** I am a source of strength and encouragement for those I care about. My love and support uplift others and create positive connections.

Embrace Financial Abundance
Develop a healthy relationship with money: Understand your financial goals and create a budget that aligns with them.
- **Affirmation:** I manage my finances responsibly, aligning my spending with my values and goals. I am a wise steward of the resources entrusted to me.

Develop valuable skills and knowledge
Investing in yourself through education or training can increase your earning potential.
- **Affirmation:** I continuously learn and grow, expanding my knowledge and skills to achieve my financial goals. My commitment to self-improvement opens doors to abundance.

Practice gratitude for what you have
Focusing on abundance, not scarcity, attracts more opportunities and blessings into your life.
• **Affirmation:** I am grateful for the abundance in my life, acknowledging that prosperity flows from a heart filled with appreciation. I share my blessings and attract even more abundance.

CHAPTER 6: Ruling Your Domain

Affirmations for Professional Success Guided by Biblical Values

Brother, shed the shackles of mere career climbers and step into the blazing light of dominion. Your professional journey isn't just about climbing the ladder; it's about wielding your skills and passion to build a kingdom of impact, guided by the unwavering compass of faith and purpose. This chapter equips you with the sacred scrolls of affirmation, empowering you to:

Achieving Career Goals

Seek the Vision Divine: Before embarking on your quest, commune with the inner oracle. Reflect on your strengths, untamed passions, and the aspirations that set your soul ablaze. Align your goals with the divine will, crafting SMART objectives that are not mere wishes, but luminous beacons guiding your path. Remember, the greatest journeys begin with a whispered prayer and a map etched with purpose.

• Affirmation: "With clarity gifted by the heavens, I set ambitious goals, fueled by the fire of faith and guided by the wisdom of the scriptures. My path unfolds, a testament to the divine plan." **(Proverbs 16:9)**

Embrace the Eternal Student

Sharpen Your Sword of Knowledge Remember, the mightiest warrior is not just strong, but ever-learning. Invest in yourself, brother. Seek out mentors, devour knowledge like a famished scholar, and hone your skills with relentless dedication. Let your mind be a fertile ground for growth, ever-receptive to new insights and strategies.

• **Affirmation:** "My mind is a boundless frontier, my spirit a boundless learner. I am a lifelong student, my thirst for knowledge unquenchable, for in wisdom lies the key to unlocking my true potential." (Proverbs 2:2-5)

Rise Above the Storm

Forging Resilience in the Crucible of Challenges Obstacles are not roadblocks, brother, but stepping stones on the path to greatness. View setbacks as opportunities to refine your strategy, bounce back with the unwavering spirit of a phoenix rising from the ashes. Remember, even the mightiest oak weathered countless storms, its roots growing stronger with each challenge.

• **Affirmation:** "Challenges are not harbingers of doom, but tests of my mettle. With unwavering faith and the resilience of a warrior, I overcome obstacles, emerging stronger and more determined." **(James 1:2-4)**

Building a Kingdom of Integrity

Lead with the Light of Righteousness

Uphold the highest ethical standards, brother. Let your business dealings be a beacon of honesty, fairness, and compassion. Remember, true prosperity is not built on exploitation, but on the foundation of righteous principles that resonate with the divine will.

• **Affirmation:** "My business prospers not through greed but stands firmly on the foundation of integrity". Justice, mercy, and humility guide my every decision, for in righteousness lies true success." (Micah 6:8)

Nurture Your Kingdom's Heart

Create a Haven of Collaboration: Foster a workplace that pulsates with respect and collaboration. Treat each employee as a valued member of your team, cmpowering them to contribute their unique talents and perspectives. Remember, a kingdom thrives on the collective strength and spirit of its people.

• **Affirmation:** "My workplace is not just a place of toil, but a haven of respect and collaboration. Each individual is valued, their voices heard, and their contributions celebrated." (Ephesians 4:29)

Share Your Bounty with the World

Extend Your Hand of Generosity: True leadership transcends mere self-interest, brother. Let your success be a source of blessing for others. Support worthy causes, uplift communities in need, and leave a legacy of positive impact that ripples outwards, touching lives far beyond your own.

• **Affirmation:** "My business is not an island, but a bridge to a better world. I share my success freely, contributing to the betterment of society and leaving a legacy that echoes through eternity." **(Proverbs 11:25)**

Break the Chains of Injustice

Conquering Barriers with Faith as Your Shield

Stand Tall, Voice unshaken: In the face of discrimination and prejudice, rise up, brother, with the courage of a lion. Be a voice for the voiceless, advocate for equality and opportunity, and challenge injustice with the unwavering conviction of your faith. Remember, true power lies not in silence, but in the righteous roar that demands change.

• **Affirmation:** "I embrace the role of a justice warrior, drawing strength from my convictions and strong faith." I stand tall against prejudice, knowing that my voice has the power to break down walls and build bridges." **(Proverbs 31:8-9)**

Embrace Your Uniqueness

Celebrate Your Divine Spark: Don't let societal norms dim your inner light, brother. Celebrate your unique identity, your talents, and the experiences that have woven the tapestry of your being. Remember, your differences are your strengths, setting you apart as a beacon of inspiration in a world that often craves conformity.

• **Affirmation:** ""I am a remarkable masterpiece, intricately crafted by the divine hand with fearful and wonderful uniqueness." I rise above prejudice, knowing my worth is inherent and my individuality a gift to the world." **(Psalm 139:14)**

Find Strength in Unity

Forge a Fellowship of Support: You are not meant to walk this path alone, brother. Seek out a community of individuals who share your values, your faith, and your aspirations. Uplift and support each other, drawing strength from your shared journey and collective wisdom. Remember, a single ember can ignite a roaring fire, and together, you can illuminate the world.

• **Affirmation:** "I am not alone. I find strength and inspiration in the community of those who believe in justice, equality, and the power of collective action. Together, we rise as a force for good, leaving an indelible mark on the world." **(Galatians 3:28)**

Leave Your Mark on the Sands of Time

Making a Ripple Effect of Change

Identify Your Sacred Cause: What sets your soul ablaze, brother? What issues tug at your heartstrings, urging you to take action? Identify your cause, the change you wish to see in the world, and let it become your guiding star. Remember, even the smallest pebble cast into the pond can create ripples that reach far and wide.

• **Affirmation:** "I am called to serve a purpose greater than myself. My talents and resources are instruments for change, leaving the world a more just and compassionate place than I found it." **(Matthew 25:35-40)**

Take Action, No Matter How Small

Change doesn't always require grand gestures, brother. Start with small, consistent actions that align with your cause. Volunteer your time, donate to worthy organizations, raise awareness, and inspire others to join you. Remember, even a single drop can eventually fill an ocean.

- **Affirmation:** "I am a catalyst for change, starting with small actions that ripple outwards to create positive change. My dedication is unwavering, knowing that even the smallest steps can lead to a brighter tomorrow." **(Proverbs 11:24-25)**

Be a Beacon of Inspiration

Let your passion be contagious, brother. Share your story, your experiences, and your vision for a better world. Inspire others to join your cause, to raise their voices, and to take action alongside you. Remember, a single flame can ignite a revolution.

- **Affirmation:** "I am a beacon of hope and inspiration, motivating others to join me in building a better world. Together, we rise as a united force, our voices echoing in unison, our actions paving the way for a brighter future." **(Matthew 5:14)**

Go forth, brother, and claim your rightful place as a force for good in the marketplace. Remember, your journey is not just about climbing the ladder of success, but about building a legacy of impact, guided by faith, purpose, and the unwavering belief that you can make a difference. As you navigate the complexities of the professional world, hold fast to your values, lead with compassion, and use your success to uplift others and leave a lasting positive impact. The world awaits your brilliance, brother. Shine forth and claim your dominion!

CHAPTER 7: Mastering Your Mind

Forging an Unbreakable Stronghold with God's Word

Brother, have you ever felt like your mind is a battlefield? Thoughts clash like swords, anxieties surge like tidal waves, and limiting beliefs whisper like insidious serpents. Fear not, warrior, for within you lies the power to transform this battlefield into an impregnable fortress. This chapter equips you with the celestial armor of self-awareness, empowering you to:

Recognizing Limiting Beliefs

Imagine shackles forged from doubt and fear, binding your potential. These are limiting beliefs, insidious whispers that masquerade as truths, often rooted in childhood experiences or societal pressures. They might sound like:

"I'm not good enough."
"I'll never achieve my dreams."
"Success is reserved for the lucky few."
Sound familiar? Don't despair! Just like Gideon unearthed hidden warriors, embark on a quest to unearth your limiting beliefs. Reflect on recurring negative thoughts:

When do they arise? What situations trigger them? How do they impact your actions and emotions? Remember, awareness is the first step to freedom. Now, challenge the narrative. Don't accept these thoughts as absolutes. Question their validity, seeking evidence to support or refute them. Remember, you are the author of your story, and you have the power to rewrite it.

• **Affirmation:** "I dismantle beliefs that hold me back, substituting them with empowering truths rooted in my faith. My mind is a fertile ground for positive growth, nourished by the wisdom of scripture. Just as David faced Goliath, I stand tall against my inner giants, knowing God's strength flows through me." **(Philippians 4:8)**

Cultivating a Growth Mindset

Imagine facing a seemingly insurmountable obstacle. The voice of negativity whispers, "Turn back, this is too hard." But a different voice, fueled by a growth mindset, whispers, "This is an opportunity to learn and grow."

Developing a growth mindset means viewing challenges not as roadblocks, but as stepping stones. Embrace them with the spirit of a learner, knowing that each obstacle holds the potential for growth and deeper understanding.

Reframe Your Perspective: Instead of asking "why is this happening to me?" ask "what can I learn from this experience?" Seek the hidden lessons within each challenge. Remember, even a diamond requires immense pressure to become its most brilliant self.

Take Joy in Small Achievements: Acknowledge and celebrate the strides you make, no matter how modest. Did you overcome a fear? Learn a new skill? Each step forward reinforces a positive growth mindset and fuels your motivation to persevere. Keep in mind, even the strongest oak tree originated from a small acorn.

- **Affirmation:** "I am committed to continuous learning, embracing challenges as valuable opportunities to broaden my knowledge and build my resilience." With each step, I grow closer to my true potential, just as a caterpillar transforms into a magnificent butterfly." **(James 1:2-4)**

Blooming Where You're Planted

Imagine a rose struggling to bloom in a barren desert. Now imagine that same rose thriving in a garden overflowing with love and nourishment. Our happiness flourishes similarly. In the midst of life's storms, cultivate a heart overflowing with gratitude.

Find joy in the simple blessings: the warmth of the sun, the laughter of a loved one, the beauty of a blooming flower. Remember, true happiness blossoms not from external circumstances, but from an inner garden nurtured by appreciation.
Practice Daily Gratitude: Start each day by acknowledging three things you're grateful for, big or small. Keep a gratitude journal to cultivate an attitude of thankfulness. Remember, even the smallest seed, watered with gratitude, can blossom into a magnificent tree.

Shift Your Focus: When negativity creeps in, consciously shift your focus to the positive aspects of your life. Look for the good, even in challenging situations. Remember, even the darkest night cannot extinguish the light of a single star.

- **Affirmation**: "My heart overflows with gratitude, attracting more blessings into my life. Even in adversity, I find joy and purpose, knowing that God's grace sustains me, just as He provided manna for the Israelites in the wilderness." **(Psalm 100:4)**

Celestial Tools for Transformation

Imagine your mind as a battlefield, but instead of clashing swords, there are verses from scripture, each one a beacon of light and truth. Scripture is your sword and shield in the battle for your mind.

Immerse yourself in God's word: Find verses that resonate with your struggles and aspirations. Use them as a sword to cut through negativity and a shield to deflect doubt. Memorize verses that offer encouragement, like:

"For I am the Lord your God, who takes hold of your right hand and says to you, 'Do not fear, I will help you.'" **(Isaiah 41:13)**

"The Lord is my light and my salvation; whom shall I fear? The Lord is the stronghold of my life; of whom shall I be afraid?" **(Psalm 27:1)**

Meditate on Scripture: Spend time contemplating inspiring verses, allowing them to penetrate your heart and mind. Let their truths reshape your thoughts and beliefs. Imagine the calming presence of Jesus as you reflect on His words.

Apply Scripture to Your Life: Seek practical ways to integrate biblical principles into your daily life. Let scripture guide your actions and decisions. Remember, faith without works is dead (James 2:17). Just as Nehemiah rebuilt the walls of Jerusalem, use scripture to rebuild the walls of your mind.

• **Affirmation:** "My mind is renewed by the power of God's word. Scripture is my guiding light, illuminating the path to truth, peace, and lasting joy. Just as the psalmist declared, 'Your word is a lamp to my feet and a light for my path,' I walk confidently, knowing God's wisdom guides me." **(Romans 12:2)**

Mastering your mind is a lifelong journey. Be patient with yourself, celebrate your progress, and never lose sight of your potential. With faith, a growth mindset, and the power of scripture as your guide, you can forge an unbreakable stronghold within your mind, ready to conquer any challenge and achieve your God-given destiny.

CHAPTER 8:
Leaving Your Mark

Building a Life of Purpose and Significance Rooted in Faith

Brother, your journey is not just about climbing the ladder of success, but about etching your name upon the sands of time. This chapter equips you to build a legacy that transcends individual achievements, leaving a kingdom of faith, purpose, and impact that ripples through generations.

Unearthing the Gem of Your Purpose

Before embarking on this noble quest, delve deep within and unearth the gem of your purpose. What sets your soul ablaze? What issues tug at your heartstrings, urging you to make a difference? Remember, true purpose lies not in external validation, but in aligning your actions with your deepest values and God's calling for your life.

- **Reflect:** Spend time in prayerful meditation, journaling, or seeking wise counsel. What are your passions, strengths, and experiences? How can you leverage them to serve a cause greater than yourself?

• **Seek Inspiration:** Draw inspiration from figures of faith who left lasting legacies, like Moses, who led his people to freedom; or Esther, who used her courage to save her people.

• **Affirmation:** "I follow a divine purpose, a radiant fire blazing within me. With unwavering faith, I seek to illuminate the world, leaving a legacy that echoes through eternity." (Proverbs 20:5)

Leading with Compassion and Justice

Your leadership extends far beyond boardrooms and deals, brother. Let compassion and justice be the cornerstones of your kingdom. Remember, true power lies not in domination, but in uplifting others and advocating for the marginalized.

• **Embrace Empathy:** Walk in the shoes of your employees, partners, and customers. Understand their needs and challenges, treating them with dignity and respect.

• **Champion Righteousness:** Stand up for what is right, even when it's difficult. Speak out against injustice and advocate for fair treatment for all. Remember, King David fought Goliath, reminding us that even the smallest can champion justice.

- **Affirmation:** "My leadership stands as a guiding light of compassion and justice, driven by the principles of love and righteousness. I strive to leave the world a more equitable and just place, following in the footsteps of leaders who led with their hearts." **(Micah 6:8)**

Empowering the Next Generation

A true king understands that his legacy extends beyond his reign. Invest in the next generation, brother. Share your wisdom, mentor young leaders, and empower them to carry the torch of faith and purpose.

- **Become a Mentor:** Seek opportunities to mentor young people, sharing your experiences and guiding them on their own journeys. Remember, Elijah passed his mantle to Elisha, ensuring the continuation of his legacy.
- **Invest in Education:** Support initiatives that equip the next generation with the knowledge and skills to make a positive impact. Remember, education is the key to unlocking potential and fostering a brighter future.
- **Affirmation:** "I serve as a bridge between generations, imparting my wisdom and faith to empower the succeeding generation in constructing a brighter world. Together, we create a legacy that

ripples through time, leaving a lasting impact on generations to come." **(Proverbs 22:6)**

Living a Life of Integrity

A king's legacy is built not just on accomplishments, but on the bedrock of integrity. Uphold the highest ethical standards in all your dealings, brother. Let your actions be a testament to your values, inspiring trust and admiration.

• **Operate with Transparency:** Conduct your business with honesty and openness. Avoid shortcuts and unethical practices, even when tempted. Remember, King Solomon's wisdom was renowned for its fairness and integrity.

• **Be a Man of Your Word:** Keep your promises and commitments, building trust and fostering strong relationships. Remember, a king's word is his bond.

• **Affirmation:** "The foundation of my kingdom is built upon integrity. I conduct myself with honesty and fairness, knowing that true success is built on a foundation of unwavering ethical principles. My legacy will be one of trust, respect, and a shining example for others to follow." (Proverbs 11:3)

Go forth, brother, and claim your rightful place as a king of faith, purpose, and impact. Remember, your legacy is not just what you achieve, but the lives you touch, the hope you inspire, and the difference you make in the world. With unwavering faith, a compassionate heart, and a commitment to integrity, you can build a kingdom that endures, leaving a lasting mark on generations to come.

BONUS

Daily Affirmation Prompts

Journaling Exercises for Personalized Bible-Based Affirmations

Welcome, brother! This section is your personal toolkit for crafting powerful, Bible-based affirmations that resonate with your unique journey. Each day, use these prompts to delve deeper into specific areas, personalize affirmations based on scripture, and record your reflections for ongoing growth. Remember, consistency is key!

Monday: Unearthing Your Purpose

Reflect: Recall a moment when you felt truly alive and purposeful. What were you doing? Who were you with? What emotions did you experience?

_____

_____

_____

Scripture: Read Proverbs 16:9

Prompt: What is one step you can take today to align your actions with your God-given purpose?

_____

_____

_____

Affirmation: "I am guided by a divine purpose, aligning my steps with God's will. With each action, I move closer to fulfilling my unique calling."

Tuesday: Cultivating Compassion and Justice

Reflect: Think of a situation where you witnessed injustice or someone in need. How did you respond? What emotions did you experience?

_____

_____

_____

Scripture: Read Micah 6:8

Prompt: Identify one action you can take today to promote justice or compassion in your community.

_____

_____

_____

Affirmation: "My heart overflows with compassion, and my actions echo with justice. I am a champion for the marginalized, following in the footsteps of those who fought for righteousness."

Wednesday: Empowering the Next Generation

Reflect: Consider an older person in your life you admire. What qualities do they possess? How have they impacted you?.

_____

_____

_____

Scripture: Read Proverbs 22:6
Prompt: Identify one way you can mentor or support a young person in your life today.

_____

_____

Affirmation: "I am a bridge between generations, sharing my knowledge and faith to empower the next generation to build a better world. Together, we create a legacy that ripples through time."

Thursday: Living with Integrity

Reflect: Recall a situation where you faced a difficult ethical choice. What did you do? How did you feel afterward?

_____

_____

_____

Scripture: Read Proverbs 11:3
Prompt: Identify one area where you can strengthen your commitment to integrity today.

_____

_____

Affirmation: "Integrity is the cornerstone of my kingdom. I conduct myself with honesty and fairness, knowing that true success is built on a foundation of unwavering ethical principles."

Friday: Weekly Reflection and Goal Setting

Reflect: Review your affirmations and journaling entries from the week. What insights did you gain? What challenges did you encounter?

_____

Scripture: Read Philippians 4:13
Prompt: Set a personalized goal for the next week that aligns with your affirmations and purpose.

Affirmation: "With God's strength and guidance, I am empowered to overcome any obstacle and achieve my goals. I move forward with unwavering faith and a renewed commitment to my journey." Remember, brother, consistency is key!

Saturday: Sabbath Rest and Gratitude

Scripture: Exodus 20:8
Reflection: What does Sabbath rest look like for you? How can you incorporate more rest and rejuvenation into your week?

Prompt: Spend time in nature, practice mindfulness, or engage in an activity that brings you peace and joy.
Affirmation: "I honor the Sabbath, allowing myself time for rest and reflection. In this stillness, I find renewed strength, gratitude, and connection to the divine."

Sunday: Worship and Renewal
Scripture: Psalm 96:9

Reflection: How does worship nourish your spirit? What faith practices bring you closer to God?

_____

_____

_____

Prompt: Attend a religious service, spend time in prayer or meditation, or engage in activities that connect you to your faith community.

Affirmation: "In the embrace of worship and community involvement, I discover a source of rejuvenation and inner fortitude. My faith serves as a guiding beacon, casting light on my journey and infusing my heart with happiness."

By dedicating time each day to reflection, journaling, and crafting personalized affirmations, you cultivate a mindset rooted in faith, purpose, and lasting impact. May your affirmations be a source of strength and inspiration as you build your kingdom of faith, compassion, and integrity.